ZAP-IT! MICROWAVE COOKBOOK

80 QUICK & EASY RECIPES

KATHERINE HUPP

DEDICATION

For My Family

INTRODUCTION

Whether one is a busy parent with little time to prepare meals, or a college student needing to cook all of their meals in a microwave oven, many people experience occasions when microwave cooking just makes sense.

Microwave cooking is fast and convenient. There is no need for the microwave to be relegated to simply heating drinks and leftovers.

With a few ingredients, a complete and tasty dish can be made right in the microwave. This cookbook contains 80 tasty recipes that can be easily cooked in a microwave oven.

Please note that power levels of different microwave ovens can vary wildly. The recipes included in this cookbook work best for a range of 1000 to 1100 watt microwave ovens. Be prepared to shorten or lengthen the cooking time as needed to suit your own particular microwave.

It is always better to undercook than to overcook. Food can always be returned to the microwave oven for further cooking. Keep a close watch on the cooking process until you understand how foods will cook in your microwave.

Contents

BASICS OF MICROWAVE COOKING
MICROWAVE SAFE UTENSILS

Ovenproof glass baking dishes, mixing bowls, measuring cups and pie plates work well in a microwave. Ceramic and china are also microwave safe. Plates and serving bowls marked ovenproof are usually acceptable for microwave cooking.

Special microwave cookware sets and dishes are also available on the market today. Silicone baking cups are inexpensive and work wonderfully when cooking muffins in the microwave oven.

When a glass lid is not available, plastic wrap can be used to tightly cover most dishes during microwave cooking. Be sure to pierce the plastic wrap to allow steam to escape. This helps to avoid being burned by steam when uncovering the dish.

Wax paper can be used to prevent splatter. Paper towels, paper cups, plates and napkins can also be used in a microwave.

Never use recycled paper products in a microwave oven. They may contain impurities which could start a fire.

Avoid all metal trimmed dishes, and remove metal ties or staples from food packages when defrosting or cooking.

MAIN DISHES
Barbeque Chicken

2 ½ to 3 pounds chicken, cut into serving pieces
½ cup tomato ketchup
2 tablespoons brown sugar
2 tablespoons apple cider vinegar
1 teaspoon prepared mustard
1 teaspoon Worcestershire sauce
½ teaspoon salt
¼ teaspoon black pepper

On a microwave safe rack, arrange chicken skin side down in a single layer. Be certain rack fits inside a shallow glass pan or baking dish to catch drippings. Optionally, chicken can be placed on an upside down glass pie plate, which fits in a glass baking dish.

In a small mixing bowl, combine ketchup, brown sugar, vinegar, Worcestershire sauce, mustard, salt and pepper. Reserve ½ cup of sauce for later use.

Spread ½ of remaining sauce over chicken. Cover with wax paper and cook on HIGH for 9 minutes. Turn chicken pieces over and rearrange placement of pieces. Spread with remaining sauce.

(continued)

Cover with wax paper and cook on HIGH 7 to 10 minutes or until juices run clear and chicken is no longer pick.

Let stand 3 minutes. Serve with remaining ½ cup sauce.

Yields 4 servings

Beef & Peppers Pasta

3 large bell peppers, coarsely chopped
1 large onion, sliced
2 tablespoons butter or margarine
1 ½ cups cooked beef, chopped
2 cups cooked elbow macaroni, drained
1 (14.5 ounce) can diced tomatoes
1 (14 ounce) jar pasta sauce

In a 2-quart glass casserole, combine peppers, onion, and butter. Cover and cook on HIGH for 4 to 5 minutes until vegetables are tender.

Add beef, macaroni, tomatoes and sauce; stir to combine. Cover and cook on HIGH for 5 to 6 minutes until heated through.

Yields 4 servings

Cheesy Tuna Casserole

1 (5 ounce) can tuna, drained
1 (10.75 ounce) can condensed cream of mushroom soup
2 cups cheddar cheese, shredded
¼ cup onion, minced or 2 teaspoons dry minced onion flakes
½ teaspoon salt
¼ teaspoon black pepper
1 ¼ cups water
2 cups instant rice

Combine all ingredients in a 2 ½-quart microwave safe baking dish; stir well. Cover with a lid or pierced plastic wrap. Cook on HIGH for 15 minutes or until set.

Yields 4 servings

Chicken & Rice Soup

2 chicken breast halves, bone-in
1 stalk celery, chopped
1 carrot, chopped
½ cup onion, chopped
3 cups chicken broth
1 cup uncooked instant rice
2 tablespoons chopped parsley

Place chicken in a 2-quart glass casserole. Cover and cook on HIGH 9 to 12 minutes or until juices run clear and chicken is no longer pink, turning chicken over after 6 minutes.

Remove chicken and allow to cool; reserve liquid. Remove bones and cut chicken breasts into small pieces.

Add 3 cups chicken broth to reserved broth in 2-quart casserole. Add celery, carrot and onion. Cover and cook on HIGH 8 minutes. Add chicken, rice and parsley; stir. Cover and cook on HIGH 4 minutes. Let stand 5 minutes until rice is softened.

Yields 4 servings

Chicken Breasts in Sour Cream Sauce

2 chicken breast halves
1 cup water
¼ teaspoon salt
6 ounces sour cream
1 (6.5 ounce) can mushroom pieces, drained
¼ cup grated parmesan cheese
¼ cup reserved chicken broth
¼ teaspoon lemon pepper

Place chicken in a 2-quart glass casserole. Add water and salt. Cover and cook on HIGH 9 to 12 minutes, turning chicken over after 6 minutes, until juices run clear and chicken is no longer pink. Drain and reserve broth. Set chicken aside to cool on a plate.

In same casserole, combine sour cream, mushrooms, parmesan cheese, chicken broth, and lemon pepper. Cut chicken into bite size pieces, and stir into sauce mixture. Cover. Cook on HIGH for 7 to 10 minutes, or until sauce begins to thicken.

Yields 2 servings

Chinese Stir-Fry

2 tablespoons cooking oil
2 cloves garlic, minced
1 teaspoon fresh ginger
¼ cup green onion, chopped
4 medium carrots, sliced
½ cup bell pepper, sliced
1 (6 ounce) package frozen pea pods
1 cup bean sprouts
2 tablespoons soy sauce
1 cup fresh mushrooms, sliced

Combine oil, garlic, ginger and onion in a 2-quart glass casserole. Cook on HIGH for 1 minute. Add carrots and green pepper. Cover and cook on HIGH for 2 ½ minutes.

Stir in pea pods, bean sprouts and soy sauce. Cover and cook on HIGH for 3 minutes. Stir in mushrooms; cover and cook on HIGH for 1 minute. Let stand 3 minutes before serving.

Yields 4 servings

Crustless Veggie Quiche

3 large eggs
1 ½ cups cheddar cheese, shredded and divided
2 tablespoons butter or margarine
1 small onion, chopped
1 (12 to 14 ounce) package frozen vegetables of your choice, thawed and drained
1 cup dry bread crumbs
¼ teaspoon salt
⅛ teaspoon black pepper
⅓ cup sour cream
Paprika (optional)

In a glass pie plate, combine butter and onion. Cook on HIGH 4 minutes or until onions are tender. Add vegetables. Cover and cook on HIGH 5 minutes. Set aside.

Combine eggs, 1 cup shredded cheese, bread crumbs, salt, pepper and sour cream. Mix well. Blend in vegetable mixture.

Pour mixture into a 9 or 10 inch glass pie plate. Arrange vegetables evenly. Top with remaining ½ cup of cheese. Sprinkle lightly with paprika. Cook on HIGH 8 to 12 minutes or until a knife inserted in center comes out clean. Let stand 2 minutes before serving.

Yields 6 to 8 servings

Easy Beef Stroganoff

1 pound beef steak, sliced thin
1 teaspoon vegetable oil
1 onion, chopped
1 to 2 cloves garlic, minced
1 (10.75 ounce) can condensed cream of mushroom soup
½ cup sour cream
¼ teaspoon black pepper

Combine steak strips, oil, onion and garlic in a 2-quart glass casserole. Cover and cook on HIGH 3 minutes; stir. Continue to cook on HIGH 2 minutes more, or until beef is no longer pink. Add soup, sour cream and pepper; stir well.

Cover and cook at 50% power 3 minutes; stir. Continue to cook at 50% power for an additional 3 minutes or until thoroughly heated. Let stand 4 minutes before serving. Serve over hot noodles.

Yields 4 to 6 servings

Easy Omelet

1 tablespoon butter or margarine
4 eggs
6 tablespoons milk
Salt and pepper to taste

In a small bowl, whisk together eggs, milk, salt and pepper.

Place butter in a round glass casserole. Cook on HIGH 30 to 50 seconds until melted. Tilt dish to coat sides with melted butter.

Pour omelet mixture into buttered casserole. Cook on HIGH for 2 minutes; stir gently and cook on HIGH for 1 to 1 ½ minutes or until done.

Yields 2 servings

Tip: Crumbled bacon, chopped ham, or shredded cheese may also be added to the egg mixture.

Yields 2 servings

Fish Fillet Amandine

4 tablespoons butter or margarine, divided
½ cup slivered almonds
1 pound fresh or frozen fish fillets, thawed
1 tablespoon lemon juice

In a small microwave proof bowl, melt 2 tablespoons butter on HIGH for 30 to 50 seconds until melted; add almonds. Cook uncovered on HIGH for 2 minutes, or until almonds are lightly toasted, stirring twice.

In a 9x9 glass baking dish, melt 2 tablespoons butter on HIGH for 30 to 50 seconds until melted. Place fish in baking dish; turn over to coat both sides with butter. Sprinkle with lemon juice.

Cover dish with vented plastic wrap and cook on HIGH for 4 to 5 minutes or until fish flakes easily with fork.

Top with toasted almonds.

Yields 4 servings

Fish Roll-ups

1 (10 ounce) package frozen chopped spinach
1 teaspoon dry minced onion
2 teaspoons lemon juice
¼ cup cream cheese, softened
¾ pound fish fillets
Paprika

Cook spinach in a glass pie plate on HIGH for 6 minutes. Drain.

In a small mixing bowl, stir together spinach, onion and lemon juice.

Evenly spread cream cheese on fish fillets. Divide spinach and spread over cream cheese. Roll up fish and secure with toothpicks. Place rollups in deep pie plate or baking dish. Sprinkle lightly with paprika.

Cover loosely with plastic wrap and cook on HIGH 4 to 7 minutes or until fish flakes easily with a fork. Remove toothpicks before serving.

Yields 4 servings

French Onion Soup

1 large onion, sliced
1 tablespoon vegetable oil
3 ½ tablespoons all-purpose flour
4 cups beef broth
2 tablespoons chopped parsley
¼ teaspoon salt
⅛ teaspoon black pepper
4 slices French bread, sliced thick
¼ cup cheese, grated and divided

Place onion and oil in a 3-quart casserole dish. Cover and cook 2 minutes. Add flour and stir to make a paste. Gradually blend in broth. Add parsley, salt and pepper. Stir until smooth.

Cover and cook on HIGH for 10 minutes, stirring once.

Pour soup into 4 microwave-safe serving bowls. Submerge bread in soup and sprinkle with ¼ of the grated cheese. Place bowls in microwave and cook on HIGH for 1 minute or until cheese is melted.

Yields 4 servings

Honey Mustard Chicken

4 boneless chicken breasts
2 tablespoons honey
1 tablespoon prepared mustard
½ teaspoon dried tarragon
1 tablespoon tomato puree or 1 tablespoon ketchup
¼ cup chicken stock
Salt and pepper to taste

Place chicken breasts in a glass casserole.

In a small bowl, mix together honey, mustard, tarragon, tomato puree and chicken stock. Pour over chicken breasts. Sprinkle with salt and pepper.

Cover and cook on HIGH for 14 to 18 minutes, rearranging and coating chicken twice during cooking time. Chicken is done when juices run clear and no longer pink inside.

Yields 4 to 6 servings

Lamb Shepherd Casserole

1 pound lamb, cubed
2 cups celery stalks, sliced
1 cup carrots, sliced
2 tablespoons butter or margarine
1 (15.25 ounce) can whole kernel corn, drained
1 (15 ounce) can cooked potatoes, drained and cubed
1 (10.75 ounce) can condensed cream of celery soup
1 (12 ounce) jar onion gravy

Place lamb in a 2-quart glass casserole. Cover and cook on HIGH for 5 minutes. Let stand 2 minutes and check for doneness; drain. Remove lamb from casserole and set aside.

In same casserole, combine celery, carrots and butter. Cover and cook on HIGH 5 to 6 minutes until vegetables are tender.

Add lamb, potatoes, corn, soup and gravy. Cover and cook on HIGH 5 to 7 minutes until heated through.

Yields 4 servings

Meatballs

1 large egg, beaten
⅓ cup milk
¼ cup quick-cooking oats
¼ bread crumbs
1 pound lean ground beef
1 small onion, chopped
1 teaspoon ground sage (optional)
1 teaspoon salt
¼ teaspoon ground black pepper

Combine egg, milk, oats and bread crumbs in a small bowl. In a medium mixing bowl, combine ground beef, onion, sage, salt and pepper. Add egg mixture and mix very well. Divide evenly and form into 24 meatballs.

Place meatballs in a 2-quart glass casserole in a single layer. Cover with paper towel. Turning meatballs twice during cooking, cook on HIGH 7 to 9 minutes until beef is no longer pink. Drain fat and let stand 4 minutes before serving.

Yields 4 servings

Meatloaf

1 (8 ounce) can tomato sauce
¼ cup brown sugar
1 teaspoon Worcestershire sauce
1 teaspoon prepared mustard
2 pounds lean ground beef
2 large eggs
1 medium onion, chopped
½ medium bell pepper, chopped
¼ teaspoon garlic powder
½ cup quick-cooking oats or cracker crumbs
¾ teaspoon salt
¼ teaspoon black pepper

Mix together tomato sauce, brown sugar, Worcestershire sauce and mustard in a small bowl. Set aside.

In a 2-quart glass baking dish, mix the ground beef, eggs, onion, green pepper, garlic powder, oatmeal, salt, black pepper and one-half of the tomato sauce mixture. Stir well to combine and press down to level top of meatloaf. Pour remaining sauce mixture evenly over top.

Cover with paper towel and cook on HIGH 10 to 15 minutes or until set and center of meatloaf is no longer pink. Drain grease. Let stand 10 minutes before serving.

Yields 6 servings

Mexican Chicken & Rice Casserole

1 pound boneless chicken strips
½ teaspoon chili powder
¼ teaspoon salt
1 tablespoon butter or margarine
1 clove garlic, minced
1 cup salsa
1 cup chicken broth
¾ cup quick cooking rice
½ cup crushed corn chips (about 1 cup uncrushed)
½ cup cheddar cheese, shredded

Sprinkle chicken with chili powder and salt. In a 1 ½-quart glass casserole, heat margarine on HIGH 30 to 40 seconds until melted. Stir in garlic, add chicken strips. Cover with paper towel to prevent splatter.

Cook on HIGH 5 to 7 minutes or until chicken is no longer pink, stirring 3 times. Add salsa, chicken broth and rice.

Cover and cook on HIGH 5 to 6 minutes or until it begins to boil. Let stand about 4 minutes until rice absorbs moisture. Stir. Top with corn chips and shredded cheese.

Do not cover. Cook on HIGH for 1 minute or until cheese is melted.

Yields 4 servings

Pepper Steak

1 pound beef steak
2 tablespoons white vinegar
1 tablespoon water
¼ cup light soy sauce
1 teaspoon garlic salt
½ teaspoon white sugar
¼ teaspoon ground ginger
1 large bell pepper, cut into strips
1 onion, sliced
2 medium fresh tomatoes, peeled and sliced
1 cup sliced fresh mushrooms
1 cup brown gravy

Slice beef into strips. In a 2-quart glass casserole, combine vinegar, water, soy sauce, garlic salt, sugar and ginger. Coat each strip of beef in seasoning mixture and add to casserole. Cover with lid and place in refrigerator to marinate for 30 minutes.

Remove from refrigerator and stir in bell pepper and onion. Cover with lid and cook on 80% power for 5 minutes or on HIGH for 3 ½ minutes. Stir in tomatoes and mushrooms.

Cover with lid and cook at 90% power for 10 to 12 minutes or on HIGH 8 to 10 minutes, or until beef is tender, stirring once halfway through cooking time.

(continued)

Stir in gravy and cook on HIGH 3 to 4 minutes until heated through. Let stand 4 minutes before serving. Serve over rice if desired.

Yields 4 servings

Poached Chicken Breasts

2 chicken breast halves
1 stalk celery, chopped
1 carrot, chopped
½ cup onion, chopped
1 cup chicken broth

Place chicken in a 2-quart glass casserole. Add remaining ingredients.

Cover with lid or plastic wrap and cook on HIGH 9 to 12 minutes, turning chicken over after 6 minutes, until juices run clear and chicken is no longer pink. Let stand 5 minutes before serving.

Yields 2 servings

Poached Eggs

2 fresh eggs
½ cup cold water
salt and pepper to taste

Pour water into a glass measuring cup or coffee cup. Add 1 cracked egg. Cover with a saucer and cook on HIGH for 30 to 45 seconds, or until egg white is cooked through and yolk is still runny. Do not overcook or yolk will explode.

Lift egg from cup onto a plate with a slotted spoon and discard water; repeat with 2nd egg. Sprinkle with salt and pepper before serving.

Yields 2 servings

Potato Soup

3 cups potatoes, diced
1 small onion, chopped
1 stalk celery, sliced
1 (13.75 ounce) can chicken broth
1 (5 ounce) can evaporated milk
2 teaspoons parsley flakes
½ teaspoon salt
½ teaspoon dried thyme (optional)
¼ teaspoon celery seed (optional)
¼ teaspoon ground black pepper

Place potatoes, onion, celery and chicken broth in a 2-quart glass casserole. Cover and cook on HIGH for 8 to 12 minutes or until potatoes are tender.

Stir in milk, parsley, salt, thyme, celery seed, and pepper. Cover and cook on HIGH 4 to 5 minutes or until heated through.

Yields 4 servings

Pork Loin & Onions

2 pounds boneless pork loin
½ cup water
3 onions, halved
1 teaspoon salt
1 teaspoon black pepper
1 teaspoon dried thyme or sage

Pierce entire pork loin with a sharp knife. Rub with salt, pepper and thyme.

Place onion halves, cut side up, in a glass pie plate. Set the pork loin on top of the onions. Pour water into pie plate.

Cover and cook on HIGH for 10 minutes. Turn the pork loin over; cover and cook on HIGH for 7 minutes. Let rest for 8 minutes before serving.

Yields 6 servings

Quick Chili

1 pound ground beef
1 medium onion, chopped
1 clove garlic, minced
1 (15.5 ounce) can chili hot beans or kidney beans
1 (15 ounce) can diced tomatoes
½ cup water
1 teaspoon salt
¼ teaspoon black pepper
Chili powder to taste

In a 2-quart glass casserole combine ground beef, onion and garlic. Cover and cook on HIGH for 5 minutes or until beef is no longer pink, stirring twice. Drain grease.

Add beans, tomatoes, water, salt, pepper and 1 to 2 teaspoons chili powder. Cover; cook on HIGH 5 minutes, stirring twice.

Yields 4 servings

Salmon Fillets with Orange Sauce

4 (4 ounce) boneless salmon fillets
2 tablespoons butter or margarine, melted
5 tablespoons orange juice
2 teaspoons cornstarch
¼ teaspoon salt
¼ teaspoon lemon pepper

In a 9-inch square glass baking dish, arrange salmon fillets with thickest parts facing the sides of the dish.

In a small microwave-safe bowl, heat butter on HIGH for 30 seconds or until melted. Add orange juice, cornstarch, salt and lemon pepper. Stir until cornstarch is dissolved. Pour over salmon.

Cover with 2 paper towels or vented plastic wrap and cook on HIGH for 6 to 8 minutes until fish flakes easily with a fork.

Yields 4 servings

Scrambled Eggs

4 eggs
¼ cup milk
¼ teaspoon salt
Dash of black pepper
1 tablespoon butter or margarine

Beat eggs, milk, salt and pepper in a bowl. Heat butter on HIGH in a deep dish glass pie plate or casserole for 30 to 40 seconds until melted. Pour egg mixture into center of dish. Do not cover.

Cook on HIGH for 1 ½ minutes. With a fork, move cooked outer edges of eggs into the center, letting uncooked eggs flow to the outer edges of dish. Cook on HIGH for 1 minute or until eggs are nearly set, stirring once. Let stand 1 minute before serving.

Yields 2 servings

Seasoned Baked Fish

1 cup seasoned dry bread crumbs
1 teaspoon lemon pepper
1 teaspoon dried parsley
½ teaspoon salt
½ cup non-flavored yogurt
1 pound fish fillets

Combine bread crumbs and seasonings in a pie plate. Coat fish with yogurt, then coat with crumb mixture.

In a 9-inch square glass baking dish, arrange fish fillets with thickest parts facing the sides of the dish. Cover with 2 paper towels and cook on HIGH for 6 to 8 minutes until fish flakes easily with a fork.

Yields 4 servings

Simple Chicken Breasts

2 chicken breast halves
1 cup water
¼ teaspoon salt

Place chicken in a 2-quart glass casserole. Sprinkle with salt and add water.

Cover and cook on HIGH 9 to 12 minutes, turning chicken over after 6 minutes, until juices run clear and chicken is no longer pink. Let stand 5 minutes before serving.

Yields 2 servings

Smoked Sausage Casserole

1 sweet potato
1 medium onion, sliced thin
3 tart apples, peeled, seeded and cubed
2 tablespoons butter or margarine
1 (12 ounce) package smoked sausage, cut into pieces
1 (12 ounce) jar pork gravy

Wash sweet potato. Pierce with fork several times and wrap in damp paper towel. Place on glass pie plate and cook on HIGH for 4 minutes. Turn sweet potato over and cook for 2 minutes more or until nearly done. Remove from microwave; cool in cold water. Remove skin and cube potato.

Place onion, apples and butter in a 2-quart glass casserole. Cover and cook on HIGH for 3 to 4 minutes or until tender. Gently stir in sweet potato, sausage and gravy.

Cover and cook on HIGH 6 to 7 minutes or until heated through.

Yields 4 servings

Sweet & Sour Pork

1 pound boneless pork, cubed
¾ cup apricot preserves
2 tablespoons prepared mustard
2 tablespoons apple cider vinegar
2 tablespoons soy sauce
1 (8 ounce) can pineapple chunks, drained
1 (8 ounce) can sliced water chestnuts, drained
1 (11 ounce) can mandarin orange slices, drained
½ cup frozen pea pods, thawed and drained
2 cups cooked rice
¼ cup sliced almonds (optional)

Place pork cubes in a 2-quart glass casserole. Cover and cook 5 to 6 minutes, stirring once. Drain.

Add apricot preserves, mustard, vinegar, soy sauce, pineapple, water chestnuts, mandarin oranges and pea pods. Cook on HIGH 2 to 4 minutes until heated through.

Serve over cooked rice. Top with sliced almonds.

Yields 4 servings

Tangy Tomato Soup

1 tablespoon butter or margarine
1 medium onion, chopped
1 large carrot, sliced into thin rings
1 large potato, chopped
1 (28 ounce) can chopped tomatoes
1 small orange, juiced
Zest of 1 orange
3 cups vegetable stock
¼ teaspoon celery seed (optional)
¼ teaspoon salt
⅛ teaspoon black pepper

In a 3-quart glass bowl or casserole, cook butter on HIGH for 30 to 40 seconds until melted. Add onion, carrot and potato. Cover and cook on HIGH for 4 minutes, stirring once.

Stir in tomatoes, orange juice, orange zest, vegetable stock, celery seed, salt and pepper. Cover and cook on high for 10 to 14 minutes, stirring twice during cooking. Soup is done when vegetables are tender.

Yields 4 to 6 servings

Vegetarian Chili

½ cup celery, chopped
1 medium onion, chopped
½ bell pepper, chopped
1 to 2 tablespoons chili powder
1 teaspoon salt
¼ teaspoon black pepper
1 (15.5 ounce) can chili beans
1 (15 ounce) can chick peas or kidney beans
1 (15 ounce) can Great Northern beans
2 (15 ounce) cans diced tomatoes

Place celery, onion and bell pepper in a 3-quart casserole dish. Cover and cook 3 to 4 minutes until tender. Add spices; stir well. Add beans and tomatoes; stir.

Cover and cook on HIGH 12 to 15 minutes or until thoroughly heated, stirring once. Stir before serving.

Yields 4 servings

Western Chicken & Rice Casserole

¾ cup chopped leftover chicken or 1 (5 ounce) can chicken chunks, drained
1 (4 ounce) can diced green chilies (optional)
1 (10.75 ounce) can condensed cream of mushroom soup
2 cups cheddar cheese, shredded
¼ cup onion, minced or 2 teaspoons dry minced onion flakes
¾ teaspoon chili powder (optional)
½ teaspoon salt
¼ teaspoon black pepper
1 ¼ cups hot water
2 cups instant rice

Combine all ingredients in a large bowl and stir well. Mixture will be somewhat soupy. Pour into a 2-quart microwave safe baking dish.

Cover with a lid or plastic wrap. Cook on HIGH for 10 to 13 minutes or until set.

Yields 4 servings

Wine-Poached Fish

1 cup dry white wine
¼ teaspoon crushed rosemary leaves
¼ teaspoon salt
⅛ teaspoon black pepper
1 pound fresh or frozen fish fillets, thawed
½ lemon, thinly sliced

Combine wine, rosemary, salt and pepper in a 9x9-inch glass baking dish. Arrange fillets in dish with thickest edges to the outside of dish. Top with lemon slices.

Cover with vented plastic wrap and cook on HIGH 4 to 6 minutes or until fish flakes easily with a fork.

Yields 4 servings

SIDE DISHES

Acorn Squash

1 acorn squash
4 teaspoons brown sugar, divided
2 teaspoons butter or margarine, divided
Cinnamon (optional)

Pierce squash several times with a knife. Place on a glass pie plate or baking dish and cook on HIGH for 5 minutes. Turn squash over and cook on HIGH for 4 additional minutes. Cut squash in half; remove seeds. Place 1 teaspoon of butter and 2 teaspoons of sugar in seed cavity of each half. Sprinkle with cinnamon.

Return to microwave, cut side up, and cook on HIGH 3 to 4 minutes or until flesh is tender.

Yields 2 servings

Baked Beans

3 slices bacon, cut into thirds
1 (16 ounce) can pork and beans
1 small onion, chopped (optional)
¼ cup ketchup
2 tablespoons brown sugar
1 teaspoon Worcestershire sauce

Place bacon in a 1-quart glass casserole and cover with lid. Cook on HIGH 2 ½ minutes. Stir in beans, onion, ketchup, sugar and Worcestershire sauce.

Cover and cook on 70% power 10 to 12 minutes, stirring occasionally.

Yields 3 to 4 servings

Broccoli & Cauliflower Salad

1 cup fresh broccoli florets
1 cup fresh cauliflower florets
½ cup mayonnaise
1 ½ teaspoons prepared mustard
½ teaspoon crushed dried basil

Place broccoli and cauliflower in a 2-quart glass casserole. Cover with lid and cook on HIGH for 3 to 4 minutes, or until tender crisp. Drain and cool.

Combine mayonnaise, mustard and basil in a small bowl. Pour over cooled vegetables and toss to mix.

Yields 4 servings

Candied Sweet Potatoes

1 ¼ pounds sweet potato (about 2 medium)
2 medium apples
¼ cup apple juice
¼ cup brown sugar, firmly packed
1 teaspoon cinnamon
2 tablespoons butter or margarine
¼ cup chopped nuts (optional)

Peel sweet potatoes and apples. Slice ¼-inch thick and layer in a 1 ½- quart glass casserole. Pour on juice.

In a small bowl, combine cinnamon and sugar and sprinkle on sweet potatoes. Dot with pieces of butter. Top with nuts.

Cover and cook on HIGH for 9 to 13 minutes until sweet potatoes are tender, stirring after 6 minutes. Let stand 2 minutes before serving.

Yields 4 servings

PLAIN SWEET POTATOES
- Peel S. Potatoe
- Slice into similar size pieces
- Put on plate + cover
- MICRO WAVE ON HIGH = 9min. to 13min. UNTIL TENDER

Cheese-Topped Baked Potatoes

2 large baking potatoes
2 tablespoons butter or margarine, divided
4 tablespoons cheddar cheese, shredded and divided
salt and pepper
6 teaspoons sour cream, divided

Wash potatoes and prick 3 times a fork. Place on a microwave-proof plate.

Cook on HIGH for 5 minutes. Turn potatoes over and cook on HIGH 5 minutes more, or until potatoes are soft. Cut potatoes in half lengthwise. Season with salt and pepper to taste. Mash center of potatoes lightly with a fork. Top with 1 tablespoon butter and 2 tablespoons cheddar cheese. Return to the microwave and cook on HIGH 30 seconds to 1 minute, or until cheese is melted.

Top with sour cream before serving.

Yields 2 servings

Corn on the Cob

2 ears sweet corn, husked and cleaned
butter to taste
salt & pepper to taste

Wrap ears of corn in damp paper towels and place on a microwave-proof plate. Cook on HIGH for 5 minutes, turning ears over after 3 minutes. Corn is done when kernels pierce easily with a fork.

While warm, add butter, salt and pepper to taste.

Yields 2 servings

Corn Muffins

1 large egg
½ cup milk
⅛ cup vegetable oil
¾ cup yellow corn meal
½ cup all-purpose flour
1 ½ teaspoons baking powder
½ teaspoon salt
⅛ cup sugar

In a medium bowl, beat egg, milk and oil. In a separate bowl, mix corn meal, flour, baking powder, salt and sugar; stir to combine. Add dry ingredients to egg mixture and stir until smooth.

Grease a microwave safe muffin pan, or use non-stick silicone cup holders without greasing. Fill each cup no more than two-thirds full. Place muffin pan or silicone cup holders directly on glass tray in microwave.

Cook on HIGH 2 to 3 ½ minutes or until tops are nearly dry to touch. Check for doneness at 2 minutes and every 30 seconds thereafter.

Yields 9 servings

Creamy Green Beans

1 (10 ounce) frozen French-style green beans
1 (10.75 ounce) can condensed cream of celery soup
1 (4 ounce) can mushroom pieces, drained
¼ cup milk
½ teaspoon soy sauce
1 (2.8 ounce) can French fried onions, divided

Place green beans in a 2-quart casserole. Cover and cook on HIGH 4 to 6 minutes or until heated through. Allow to stand for 2 minutes; drain. Stir in soup, mushrooms, milk and soy sauce.

Cover and cook on HIGH for 4 to 5 minutes or until thoroughly heated. Stir in ½ of onions. Continue to cook covered on HIGH for 4 to 5 minutes. Top with remaining onions and cook for 1 minute. Remove cover and let stand 2 minutes before serving.

Yields 4 servings

Glazed Baby Carrots

1 pound peeled baby carrots
2 tablespoons butter or margarine
1 tablespoon brown sugar (light or dark)
½ teaspoon ground cinnamon

Place all ingredients in a 1 ½-quart glass casserole. Cover and cook on HIGH 8 to 10 minutes or until carrots are tender, stirring every 2 minutes. Let stand 2 minutes before serving.

Yields 4 servings

Harvard Beets

1 can sliced beets
¼ cup white sugar
1 tablespoon cornstarch
¼ teaspoon salt
Dash ground cinnamon (optional)
Dash ground cloves (optional)
3 tablespoons orange juice
2 tablespoons apple cider vinegar

Drain beets and reserve ½ cup juice.

In a 1-quart glass casserole, combine sugar, cornstarch, salt and spices. Mix in orange juice, vinegar and beet juice. Stir until cornstarch is dissolved.

Microwave on HIGH for 1 ½ to 2 ½ minutes, or until mixture is clear and slightly thickened, stirring once. Add beets and stir gently to coat with sauce. Cover and cook on HIGH 2 to 4 minutes until beets are heated through.

Yields 4 servings

Jalapeno Salad

1 ½ cups shredded cabbage
½ cup shredded carrots
½ medium bell pepper, sliced into thin 1-inch long strips
½ cup cherry tomatoes, cut in half
¼ cup sliced green onion
2 tablespoons fresh cilantro, chopped
¼ cup Pepper/Jack cheese, cubed
3 ounces cream cheese, softened
1 tablespoon white vinegar

Combine the cabbage, carrots, bell pepper, tomatoes, green onion and cilantro in a 1 ½-quart glass casserole ; set aside.

Combine cheese cubes, creamed cheese and vinegar in a 1-quart microwave-safe bowl. Stir well. Place in microwave and cook at 30% power 3 to 4 minutes, stirring twice during cooking. Cook on HIGH for 1 minute; stir. Let stand 2 minutes and stir until smooth. Pour cheese over vegetables and stir gently to coat.

Cover with lid and cook on HIGH 3 minutes or until heated through, stirring once during cooking. Let stand 2 minutes before serving.

Yields 4 servings

Macaroni & Cheese

1 cup uncooked elbow macaroni
4 cups hot water
½ teaspoon salt
2 tablespoons butter or margarine
¼ cup onion, chopped (optional)
2 tablespoons all-purpose flour
½ teaspoon dry mustard (optional)
¼ teaspoon salt
⅛ teaspoon black pepper
1 ¼ cups milk
1 ½ cups cheddar cheese, shredded

In a 2-quart casserole dish, combine macaroni, water and ½ teaspoon salt. Do not cover. Cook on HIGH 4 to 5 minutes. Stir. Cook an additional 4 to 5 minutes on HIGH until macaroni is al dente. Drain and rinse with hot water in a colander. Set aside.

In same casserole, heat butter on HIGH 30 to 40 seconds or until melted. Add onion and cook on HIGH for 1 minute, or until tender.

Add flour, mustard, salt and pepper. Stir to form a paste. Gradually stir in milk until smooth. Cook on HIGH for 3 to 4 minutes until sauce boils and thickens, stirring after each minute of cooking. Stir in cheese. Cook 1 minute on HIGH. (continued)

Stir macaroni in cheese sauce and mix well. Cook uncovered on HIGH 3 to 4 minutes until macaroni is heated through, stirring once. Let stand 1 minute before serving. Yields 4 servings

Pecan & Cracker Stuffed Acorn Squash

1 acorn squash (about 1 pound)
2 ¾ tablespoons butter or margarine
⅓ cup butter-cracker crumbs
¼ cup chopped pecans
2 tablespoons brown sugar
¼ teaspoon salt
Cinnamon for sprinkling

Pierce squash several times with a knife. Place on a glass pie plate or baking dish and cook on HIGH for 5 minutes. Turn squash over and cook on HIGH for 4 additional minutes. Cut squash in half; remove seeds.

In a small microwave-safe bowl, melt butter for 30 to 40 seconds on HIGH. Mix in cracker crumbs, pecans, brown sugar and salt. Fill each seed cavity with crumb mixture. Cover with wax paper.

Return to microwave, cut side up, and cook on HIGH 3 to 4 minutes or until flesh is tender. Remove wax paper and allow to stand for 4 minutes. Sprinkle lightly with cinnamon before serving. Yields 2 servings

Simple Spanish Rice

1 cup long grain white rice
1 ¼ cups hot water
1 cup salsa

In 2 ½-quart glass casserole combine rice, water and salsa. Stir. Cover with lid and cook on HIGH for 5 minutes; stir.

Cover with lid and cook at 50% power for 15 minutes. Let stand covered for 5 minutes. Fluff with fork before serving.

Spiced Garbanzo Beans

½ tablespoon vegetable oil
1 small onion, chopped
1 clove garlic, minced
1 small piece ginger root, grated
1 teaspoon ground coriander
1 teaspoon chili powder
¼ teaspoon turmeric
¼ teaspoon salt
1 (14.5 ounce) can diced tomatoes
1 green chili, seeded and chopped
4 cardamoms, crushed
2 sprigs fresh coriander, chopped
1 bay leaf
1 (15 ounce) canned chickpeas, ½ liquid reserved
1 lemon, juiced

In a 2 ½-quart glass casserole, combine oil, onion, garlic, ginger, coriander, chili powder, turmeric and salt. Cook on HIGH for 1 ½ minutes. Add tomatoes, chilies, cardamoms, coriander, bay leaf, chickpeas, reserved liquid and lemon juice; stir.

Cover and cook on HIGH for 4 to 7 minutes or until completely heated through, stirring once during cooking time. Remove bay leaf and serve.

Yields 6 servings

Tropical Yams

2 (18 ounce) cans yams or sweet potatoes, drained
1 (8.5 ounce) can crushed pineapple
½ cup melted butter or margarine
¼ cup granulated sugar
1 teaspoon cinnamon
½ cup pecans, chopped
¼ cup brown sugar

In 2-quart glass casserole, mash yams with pineapple, butter, granulated sugar, and cinnamon. Cook on HIGH for 4 to 6 minutes; stir.

Sprinkle pecans and brown sugar evenly over top. Microwave on HIGH for 2 to 4 minutes until topping is melted.

Yields 6 servings

White Rice

1 cup long-grain white rice
2 cups hot water
1 teaspoon butter or margarine
1 teaspoon vanilla (optional)
¼ teaspoon salt

In a 2 ½-quart glass casserole, combine rice, hot water, butter, vanilla and salt. Cover with lid and cook on HIGH for 5 minutes. Stir.

Cover with lid and cook at 50% power for 15 minutes, or until moisture is absorbed. Remove casserole from microwave.

Fluff with fork. Replace lid and let stand 3 minutes before serving.

Yields 4 servings

Wilted Spinach Salad

6 slices bacon
¼ cup bacon dripping or vegetable oil
½ pound fresh spinach
2 tablespoons white sugar
2 tablespoons apple cider vinegar

Arrange bacon on a microwave rack or microwave proof plate and cover with a paper towel. Cook on HIGH 4 to 5 minutes, or until bacon is crisp. Drain ¼ cup of drippings into a microwave-safe bowl. Add sugar and vinegar; stir. Set aside.

Wash spinach, pat dry, and place in a serving bowl. Crumble bacon and top spinach with crumbles.

Cook drippings mixture on HIGH for 1 minute or until it boils. Stir and pour over spinach. Serve immediately.

Yields 4 servings

Tip: The same method can be used for making Wilted Lettuce

DESSERTS & CANDY

Blueberry Muffins

⅓ cup fresh or frozen blueberries, thawed
⅔ cup all-purpose flour
3 tablespoons granulated sugar
1 teaspoon baking powder
⅛ teaspoon salt
1 egg, beaten
¼ cup milk
2 tablespoons vegetable oil
2 tablespoons brown sugar
½ teaspoon ground cinnamon

In a medium mixing bowl, combine flour, sugar, baking powder, and salt. Form a well in center of dry mixture.

Crack egg in a small mixing bowl and beat slightly. Add milk and oil. Stir and add to dry ingredients, stirring just enough to moisten mixture. Gently fold in blueberries.

Grease a microwave-safe muffin pan, or line with paper baking cups. Silicone baking cups may also be used. Fill each cup with mixture no more than half full.

Combine brown sugar and cinnamon in a small bowl. Sprinkle on top of muffin batter.

Cook on HIGH for 2 to 3 ½ minutes or until tops are nearly dry to the touch. Yields 6 servings

Brownies

2 eggs
1 cup white sugar
½ teaspoon salt
1 teaspoon vanilla
½ cup butter or margarine, melted
½ cup baking cocoa
¾ cup all-purpose flour
1 cup chopped nuts (optional)

In a medium mixing bowl, beat together the eggs, brown sugar, salt and vanilla until frothy. In a small microwave safe bowl, cook butter on HIGH 30 to 40 seconds or until melted. Stir melted butter into egg mixture.

Gradually beat in flour and cocoa until well blended. Stir in nuts. Spread evenly in a well-greased 8x8 or 9x9-inch baking dish.

Microwave on HIGH 3 to 7 minutes, checking for doneness at 3 minutes and every 30 seconds thereafter, or until a sunken moist area approximately 1 ½ inches across remains in the center. Do not overcook or brownies will be hard and dry.

Allow to cool before cutting. Brownies should be moist in the center and chewy on the outside.

Yields 9 servings

Cherry Cheesecake

¼ cup butter or margarine
1 teaspoon granulated sugar
1 cup crushed graham crackers or crushed gingersnaps
2 (8 ounce) packages cream cheese, softened
½ cup granulated sugar
1 tablespoon lemon juice
1 teaspoon vanilla
2 eggs
1 (15 ounce) can cherry pie filling

In a 9-inch deep dish glass pie plate, cook butter on HIGH 30 to 40 seconds or until melted. Stir in 1 teaspoon sugar. Add graham cracker crumbs and stir with fork. Press mixture onto bottom and sides of pie plate. Cook on HIGH for 2 minutes. Set aside.

In a medium bowl, stir together cream cheese, sugar, lemon juice, and vanilla. Add eggs and beat until well blended. Pour into prepared pie crust.

Cook on HIGH 6 to 8 minutes or until center is almost set. Let stand 5 minutes.

Place in refrigerator to chill before topping with pie filling.

Yields 8 servings

Cherry Surprise

½ cup granulated sugar
½ cup self-rising flour, sifted
1 (15 ounce) can cherry pie filling
½ teaspoon almond extract
¼ teaspoon cinnamon
4 tablespoons butter or margarine, melted

In a small bowl, sift together sugar and self-rising flour. Set aside.

Pour pie filling into 9x9-inch glass baking dish. Sprinkle with almond extract and cinnamon. Sprinkle sifted sugar and flour over filling. Pour melted butter over top.

Cook on HIGH for 10 to 13 minutes.

Tip: Apple or blueberry pie filling may be substituted for cherry pie filling.

Chocolate Fudge

4 cups powdered sugar
½ cup baking cocoa powder
¼ cup milk
½ cup butter
2 teaspoons vanilla

Butter a 9x9-inch baking dish; set aside.

In a medium glass bowl, stir together powdered sugar and cocoa. Pour milk over mixture and place butter on top. Cook on HIGH until butter is melted for 1 to 1 ½ minutes. Stir in vanilla and beat until smooth. Pour into buttered baking dish.

Chill in refrigerator before cutting into pieces. Store in refrigerator.

Yields 12 to 16 pieces

Chocolate Pudding

½ cup granulated sugar
⅓ cup baking cocoa powder
3 tablespoons cornstarch
⅛ teaspoon salt
2 cups whole milk
2 teaspoons vanilla

In a medium glass bowl, mix sugar, cocoa, cornstarch and salt. Gradually stir in milk until all lumps are dissolved.

Cook uncovered on HIGH for 3 minutes; stir. Cook on HIGH for 2 to 5 minutes, or until shiny and thick, stirring every 1 minute. Stir in vanilla.

Cover and chill in refrigerator before serving.

Yields 4 servings

Coffee Cake

1 ½ cups all-purpose flour
1 ¾ teaspoons baking powder
¾ teaspoon salt
1 tablespoon plus 1 ½ teaspoons shortening
¼ cup white sugar
½ cup milk
1 egg
2 tablespoons oil
⅓ cup all-purpose flour
⅓ cup packed brown sugar
2 tablespoons butter or margarine, room temperature
1 teaspoon cinnamon
¾ cup powdered sugar (optional)
1 tablespoon milk (optional)

Grease or line an 8-inch round microwave-safe baking dish with wax paper. Set aside.

In a medium mixing bowl, combine flour, baking powder and salt. Cut in shortening and sugar until coarse. Add milk, egg, and oil. Mix well. Pour into prepared dish.

In a small mixing bowl, combine flour, brown sugar, butter, and cinnamon. Mix until crumbly. Sprinkle evenly over batter.
(continued)

Microwave on HIGH for 4 to 8 minutes or until toothpick inserted near center comes out clean.
Cool and drizzle with a glaze made by stirring powdered sugar and milk together, if desired.

Yields an 8-inch 1 layer cake

Glazed Black Walnuts

1 stick butter or margarine
1 cup brown sugar, packed
1 teaspoon cinnamon
4 cups black walnut halves or pieces

In a 1 ½-quart glass casserole heat butter on HIGH 30 to 40 seconds until melted. Stir in brown sugar and cinnamon. Cook on HIGH for 2 minutes. Mix well.

Add walnuts and stir until well coated. Cover with a paper towel and cook on HIGH 3 to 5 minutes. Spread on wax paper or baking sheet to cool.

Yields 1 pound

Oatmeal Chocolate Bars

1 cup butter or margarine, room temperature
1 ½ cups quick-cooking oats
½ cup all-purpose flour
1 cup packed brown sugar
2 eggs
1 cup chopped nuts
1 teaspoon vanilla
2 cups semi-sweet chocolate chips, divided

Grease an 8x8-inch glass baking dish. Set aside.

In large mixing bowl, mix butter, oats, flour, sugar, eggs, nuts and vanilla. Beat until mixture is light and fluffy. Stir in 1 cup chocolate chips.

Spread batter into prepared dish. Cover with wax paper.

Cook on HIGH power 4 to 6 ½ minutes until top is almost dry to touch. Remove from microwave and sprinkle remaining chocolate chips evenly over top.

Let stand 10 minutes while chocolate chips melt; spread melted chocolate over bars. Cool before slicing into bars.

Yields 9 bars

Peanut Brittle

1 ½ cups salted or dry roasted peanuts
1 cup granulated sugar
½ cup light corn syrup
⅛ teaspoon salt (optional)
1 teaspoon butter or margarine
1 teaspoon vanilla
1 teaspoon baking soda

Butter a cookie sheet; set aside.

In a medium glass bowl, combine sugar, corn syrup, and salt. Cook uncovered on HIGH for 3 ½ minutes. Stir in peanuts and cook on HIGH for 3 minutes. Stir in butter and vanilla and cook on HIGH for 1 minute.

Stir in baking soda very quickly, just until mixture is foamy. Quickly pour onto buttered cooking sheet and spread thin. Let cool and break into serving size pieces.

Yields 1 pound

Peanut Butter Fudge

¾ cup butter or margarine
1 cup creamy peanut butter
1 ½ teaspoons vanilla
4 cups (1 pound) powdered sugar

In a large glass bowl, heat butter and peanut butter on HIGH for 2 minutes, or until easy to stir. Blend well and stir in vanilla.

Gradually stir in powdered sugar until smooth and all lumps have disappeared. Pour into a buttered 9x9-inch baking dish.

Cool in refrigerator before cutting into pieces.

Yields 16 servings

Pineapple Upside-Down Cake

⅓ cup brown sugar
2 tablespoons butter or margarine
1 (8 ounce) can crushed pineapple, drained, ¼ cup juice
reserved
10 maraschino cherries
4 tablespoons butter or margarine, room temperature
½ cup granulated sugar
1 egg
1 cup self-rising flour
1 ½ teaspoons ground cinnamon
½ teaspoon ground ginger

Grease the sides of a 2-quart round glass baking dish and
line the bottom with wax paper.

Sprinkle the brown sugar over bottom and dot with 2
tablespoons butter. Arrange maraschino cherries in bottom.
Spread crushed pineapple evenly over bottom of dish.

In a medium mixing bowl, cream granulated sugar and 4
tablespoons butter. Mix in egg.

In a separate bowl, sift together flour, cinnamon and ginger.
Add to wet ingredients alternately with ¼ cup reserved
pineapple juice. Pour batter carefully into baking dish.
(continued)

Cook on HIGH 4 to 6 minutes until top of cake is almost dry when touched.

Let stand 5 minutes. Turn onto a plate and serve warm or cool.

Raisin Spice Cake

1 ¼ cups raisins, chopped
¾ cup brown sugar
¾ cup water
½ cup shortening
¼ cup molasses or honey
1 teaspoon cinnamon
½ teaspoon nutmeg
¼ teaspoon cloves
1 ¾ cups all-purpose flour
1 teaspoon baking soda

Grease a 3-quart round glass casserole or heavy glass bowl. Set aside.

In a medium glass mixing bowl, combine raisins, brown sugar, water, shortening, molasses, cinnamon, nutmeg and cloves. Cook on high for 4 to 6 minutes or until mixture begins to boil.

While mixture cools slightly, mix flour and baking soda in a small bowl. Add to cooled mixture and stir well. (continued)

Pour into a prepared dish and cook on HIGH power 4 to 6 ½ minutes until top is almost dry to touch. Let stand 5 minutes.

Yields 8 servings

Rocky Road Candy

2 (8 ounce) packages semi-sweet chocolate chips
1 (15 ounce) can sweetened condensed milk
1 (10 ounce) package miniature marshmallows
½ cup chopped nuts

Butter a 9x13-inch baking dish. Set aside.

In a 2-quart glass casserole, heat chocolate on HIGH for 4 to 6 minutes until melted. Stir until smooth. Quickly stir in sweetened condensed milk, marshmallows and nuts, blending well.

Spread mixture into prepared dish and refrigerate before cutting.

Yields 2 ½ pounds

Spice Cake

⅔ cup all-purpose flour
2 teaspoons baking cocoa powder
¼ teaspoon baking powder
¼ teaspoon baking soda
1 ½ teaspoons ground cinnamon
1 teaspoon ground ginger
¼ teaspoon ground nutmeg
¼ teaspoon ground cloves
⅓ cup packed brown sugar
2 eggs
4 tablespoons oil
2 tablespoons honey
⅓ cup water
Powdered sugar (optional)

Grease a 2-quart round glass casserole or heavy glass bowl. Set aside.

In a medium mixing bowl, combine flour, cocoa, baking powder, baking soda, cinnamon, ginger, nutmeg, cloves and brown sugar. Mix until spices are well combined.

Stir in eggs, oil, honey, water and egg. Beat well. Pour into prepared dish.

Microwave on HIGH for 3 to 5 minutes, or until top is nearly dry and springs back slightly when touched.

(continued)

Let stand 5 minutes. Turn onto a plate and serve warm or cool. Dust with powdered sugar, if desired.

Yields 6 servings

Yellow Cake

½ cup butter or margarine, room temperature
½ cup granulated sugar
1 egg
1 teaspoon vanilla
½ cup self-rising flour, sifted
2 ½ tablespoons milk

Grease the sides and line the bottom of an 8-inch microwave-safe round dish with wax paper. Set aside.

In a medium mixing bowl, cream the butter and sugar together until light and fluffy. Beat in the egg and vanilla. Blend in sifted flour alternately with milk. Beat well.

Pour into prepared baking dish. Cook on HIGH for 3 to 6 minutes, until a toothpick inserted near center comes out clean.
Turn out onto a plate and cool before frosting, or dust with powdered sugar and serve warm.

Yields an 8-inch one layer cake

SAUCES & DIPS

Brown Gravy

1 tablespoon fat drippings
1 tablespoon all-purpose flour
½ cup water
½ cup milk

In a 1-quart glass mixing bowl, combine drippings and flour. Stir into a paste. Gradually stir in liquid until no lumps remain.

Cover and cook on HIGH 3 to 4 minutes, stirring every 30 seconds, until thickened as desired. Let stand 2 minutes before serving.

Yields 1 cup

Cheese Sauce

2 tablespoons butter or margarine
2 tablespoons all-purpose flour
½ teaspoon salt
½ teaspoon dry mustard
⅛ teaspoon white pepper
1 ¼ cups milk
1 ½ cups Cheddar cheese, shredded

In a 1-quart glass casserole or microwave safe bowl heat butter 30 to 40 seconds until melted. Stir in flour, salt, mustard, and pepper until well blended.

Gradually add milk, stirring well. Do not cover. Cook on HIGH 3 to 3 ½ minutes or until mixture boils, stirring each minute. Stir in shredded cheese.

Cook on HIGH for 30 seconds or until cheese is melted. Stir before serving.

Yields 2 ¾ cups

Cheese Spread

1 (8 ounce) package cream cheese
½ cup green onions, chopped
1 cup carrots, shredded
2 teaspoons lime or lemon juice
1 cup Monterey Jack cheese, shredded
4 tablespoons sliced almonds (optional)

Place cream cheese, onions, carrots and juice in a 2-quart casserole dish.

Cook uncovered on HIGH for 1 to 2 minutes until cream cheese is softened. Add shredded cheese and stir until well combined. Top with almonds. Serve on crackers or on toasted bread.

Yields 4 servings

Cheesy Nacho Dip

½ onion, chopped
2 tablespoons butter or margarine
1 (16 ounce) package processed cheese food, cubed
1 (8 ounce) jar salsa
2 tablespoons cilantro, chopped

In a 1-quart casserole, heat butter 30 to 40 seconds or until melted. Add onion and cook on HIGH for 1 to 2 minutes until tender. Add cheese food, salsa and cilantro.

Heat on HIGH 5 to 6 minutes or until cheese is melted, stirring twice during cooking time.

Serve with tortilla chips, crackers, or vegetable sticks.

Yields 3 cups

Chili Cheese Dip I

1 (16 ounce) package processed cheese food, cubed
1 (15 ounce) can chili with beans

Combine cheese food and chili in a in a 1-quart casserole. Cover and heat on HIGH for 3 minutes. Stir and continue to heat on HIGH for an additional 2 to 3 minutes until cheese is thoroughly melted. Stir well to combine before serving.

Serve with tortilla chips, crackers, vegetable sticks, or on toasted bread.

Yields 4 cups

Chili Cheese Dip II

1 (15 ounce) can chili with beans
1 teaspoon chili powder
1 (8 ounce) package cream cheese, room temperature
1 cup cheddar cheese, shredded

In a small mixing bowl, mix chili and chili powder thoroughly.

Spread cream cheese in the bottom of a 9-inch glass pie plate. Spread chili mixture evenly over cream cheese. Sprinkle cheese evenly over top of chili. Heat on HIGH for 3 to 5 minutes until cheese is melted.
Yields 4 cups

Hollandaise Sauce

2 egg yolks
½ teaspoon lemon juice
1 tablespoon mayonnaise
Dash cayenne pepper
¼ cup butter or margarine, melted

In a small glass mixing bowl, beat egg yolks, lemon juice, mayonnaise, and cayenne pepper until smooth. Whisk melted butter into the egg yolk mixture gradually. Beat well.

Heat uncovered on HIGH for 10 seconds; whisk. Again, heat uncovered on HIGH for 10 seconds and whisk, or until sauce thickens as desired. Whisk again before serving.

Yields 2 servings

Hot Fudge Sauce

1 cup semi-sweet chocolate chips
½ cup light corn syrup
¼ cup butter or margarine
1 (14 ounce) can sweetened condensed milk
1 teaspoon vanilla
Pinch salt

In a 1-quart glass mixing bowl, combine chocolate chips, corn syrup, and butter. Heat on HIGH for 45 seconds to 1 minute, or until chocolate is melted; stir. Blend the sweetened condensed milk, vanilla and salt into the mixture. Stir well. Heat on HIGH for 1 minute; stir. Cool slightly.

Serve over ice cream, or use as a glaze for cake. Cover and store unused sauce in refrigerator. Heat on HIGH for up to 1 minute to reheat.

Pasta Sauce

1 (29 ounce) can tomato sauce
1 teaspoon Italian seasoning
1 teaspoon sugar
¼ teaspoon garlic powder
¼ teaspoon ground black pepper

Combine all ingredients in a 2-quart glass casserole or microwave safe bowl. Do not cover.

Cook on HIGH 6 to 7 minutes until mixture begins to boil. Let stand 2 minutes.

Yields 4 cups

Quick Nacho Cheese Dip

1 (16 ounce) package processed cheese food, cubed
1 (10 ounce) can diced tomatoes & green chilies, undrained
1 teaspoon lemon juice (optional)

In a 1-quart casserole dish, combine ingredients. Heat on HIGH 5 to 6 minutes or until cheese is melted, stirring twice.

Serve with tortilla chips, crackers, or vegetable sticks.

Tip: One (10.75 ounce) can of condensed cheddar cheese soup may be substituted for the processed cheese food.

Spinach & Artichoke Dip

2 tablespoons chopped onion
1 bell pepper, chopped
1 clove garlic, minced
1 (14 ounce) can artichoke hearts, drained and chopped fine
1 (10 ounce) package chopped spinach, thawed and drained
1 (8 ounce) package cream cheese, room temperature
1 tablespoon lemon juice
½ teaspoon seasoned salt
¼ teaspoon hot pepper sauce

Place onion, bell pepper and garlic in a 2-quart casserole dish. Do not cover.

Cook on HIGH 3 minutes or until bell pepper is slightly cooked but still crisp. Squeeze excess moisture from spinach. Add spinach and remaining ingredients to pepper mixture and blend well. Best served warm. Serve with crackers or vegetable sticks.

Yields 3 cups

Sweet & Sour Sauce

¾ cup apricot preserves
1 (6 ounce) can pineapple juice
2 tablespoons apple cider vinegar
1 tablespoon Dijon mustard
1 tablespoon soy sauce
2 tablespoons cornstarch

Combine all ingredients in a 1-quart glass casserole or microwave safe bowl; mix well. Do not cover.

Cook on HIGH 6 to 7 minutes, stirring twice, until sauce is thickened.

Yields 1 ¼ cups

White Sauce

2 tablespoons butter or margarine
2 tablespoons all-purpose flour
½ teaspoon salt
1 ¼ cups milk

In a 1-quart glass casserole or microwave safe bowl heat butter on HIGH for 30 to 40 seconds until melted. Stir in flour and salt until well blended.

Gradually add milk, stirring well. Do not cover. Cook on HIGH 2 to 3 ½ minutes or until mixture boils, stirring each minute. Stir before serving.

Yields 1 ¼ cups

Tip: Herbs of choice may also be added for a flavorful white sauce.

ABOUT THE AUTHOR

Katherine Hupp is a native of West Virginia and lives in the rolling foothills of the Appalachian Mountains. She is a wife, mother and grandmother and enjoys country life. She spends much of her time gardening, cooking, canning and raising animals. Her hobbies include reading, writing, crocheting and stained glass.

Other books by Katherine Hupp that you may enjoy:

1) Waffle Recipes: Wonderful Waffles and Syrups Cookbook

2) Everything Zucchini Recipes Cookbook: Zucchini Breads, Muffins, Main Dishes, Desserts, Jams & Marmalade

3) MUFFINS: 50 Appetizing Muffin Recipes with Nutritional Information

4) Perfect Pie and Pastry Recipes: Homemade Dessert Pies Made Easy Cookbook

5) Satisfying Slow Cooker Recipes: 41 Easy Crock Pot & Slow Cooker Dishes Cookbook

6) Raising Backyard Chickens From Eggs To Egg Layers

7) Names For Cats and Kittens: More Than 2000 Names For Male and Female Felines

If you enjoyed this cookbook, please take the time to drop by Amazon.com and leave feedback for the author. It's the only form of advertising available to many independent authors and it is greatly appreciated.

INDEX

SAUCES & DIPS

SIDE DISHES

CPSIA information can be obtained
at www.ICGtesting.com
Printed in the USA
LVHW100849250621
691115LV00010BB/528

9 781497 384781